What's the Deal with Estate Planning?

By

PEGGY R. HOYT, J.D., M.B.A

Contents

CHAPTER ONE

Why is Estate Planning Important?

*It's never too early to plan, because, you never know when it **will** be too late.*

Americans are optimistic.

Have you ever heard someone say, "W*hen* I win the lottery," and "*If* I die?" It's the way we think—someday we are all going to be rich and none of us is ever going die. Even in a perfect world, these would be lofty goals. The reality is that few of us will ever win the lottery or even inherit significant amounts of money and none of us will get out of here alive. It's no wonder, however, that we are hesitant to think about, talk about and plan for those events in our lives that are inevitable and have real potential for creating unnecessary grief and expense for our family.

"I don't have anything." Often, this is the response when a conversation about estate planning starts.

The truth is, you have more than you think.

First, you have people you love. In addition, you may have a home, some financial assets, a retirement plan, possibly a life insurance policy or annuity and some personal property. You may have pets that are important to you. Everyone has someone or something they need to plan for. Many people believe an "estate plan" is having a will, but it's more expansive than that.

Who has an estate plan? Everyone!

That's because if you don't create your own estate plan, your state of residence is happy to create one for you. Sadly, it is rarely the plan you would create for yourself if you had the education and tools necessary to make well-informed decisions. Hopefully that's why you are reading this book—for the purpose of educating yourself about your estate planning options.

You might be surprised to learn that most estate plans don't work. If you've ever heard someone say about a loved one who passed away, "Boy if they only knew what was going on, they would be rolling over in their grave!" then you've experienced the classic expression regarding an estate plan that didn't work. Something went wrong. What that something was could be any one of a variety of things—perhaps an unwanted probate, unexpected taxes, unintended beneficiaries, unequal distributions, business succession issues, family hostility, and the list goes on.

A primary goal of estate planning should be to create a plan that works—for you and for your family. No two families are alike and as a result, no two plans will ever be alike.

Estate planning is not for the faint of heart and should never be left to a form found online—there are too many unexpected and potentially devastating consequences. Contrary to what you may have heard, there is no boilerplate "one size fits all" when it comes to estate planning.

Estate planning implicates many other areas of the law. These can include family law, real estate law, banking law, homestead law, guardianship law, probate and trust administration law, tax law, asset protection law and contract law, to name a few. Unless you're an expert in each of these areas of the law and know how they affect your family, then getting a professional on your team will increase the likelihood of creating a plan that will work for you and your family.

Every day you meet well-meaning individuals and professionals that will inadvertently give you estate planning advice. You'll find them in the form of realtors, bankers, financial advisors, insurance agents, title agents and car sales personnel, just to mention a few. For example, when you open a bank account, you might be asked for ownership instructions or a beneficiary designation. This is where the trouble begins. How you title your account and who you name as beneficiary should be consistent with your intended estate plan or you may be creating problems down the road.

Your estate plan should be designed to accomplish a variety of goals.

For instance, what happens if you become mentally disabled during your lifetime? Statistics indicate we are more likely to become disabled for a period of time, rather than just "simply" dying.[1]

And, at the time of death, what are your goals? Avoiding probate shouldn't be your only goal. Protecting your family

_____
1 http://www.disabilitycanhappen.org/chances_disability/disability_stats.asp

and making sure your assets are distributed when, how and to whom you want should be a central focus.

Remember, it's your family, your loved ones, and your wishes and goals.

The best course of action starts with working with a qualified legal professional who has expertise and experience in estate planning and elder law—and someone who will listen, answer your questions and help you understand how your plan will work. Only then can you have certainty that your plan has the greatest probability of success.

CHAPTER TWO

Should I Plan for Mental Disability?

No book on estate planning would be complete without a conversation about mental disability. As a nation, we are living longer.[2] Living longer may mean more health related issues, including the loss of mental capacity. As a result, a key opening question is, "Who will make legal and health care decisions for you if you can't make them for yourself?"

What would happen if tomorrow you were involved in a car accident that wasn't your fault, but that resulted in serious injury, including a coma? Are you prepared?

Without a Health Care Power of Attorney (Health Care Surrogate) there will be no one legally appointed to make medical care decisions for you. Without a Durable Financial Power of Attorney there will be no one legally appointed to make legal and financial decisions for you. The results could be catastrophic. Likely, your family will be forced to subject you (and your assets) to a guardianship proceeding.

---

2 Healthy life expectancy for 187 countries, 1990–2010: a systematic analysis for the Global Burden Disease Study 2010" by Joshua A. Salomon, et al., Institute for Health Metrics and Evaluation.

A guardianship is one of the worst kinds of lawsuits. It's one your family files against you, you get to pay for it, and ultimately, you lose. A judge makes a life changing determination for you—whether you are mentally competent, who will be your guardian and what that person can do with you and your money. A guardianship is expensive, time consuming and lasts for the rest of your life or until you regain mental capacity (which is often not very likely).

Without proper mental disability planning you may be at the mercy of the guardianship court.

A Health Care Power of Attorney allows you to appoint those persons you want to make your health care related decisions. If you are married, it will likely be your spouse. If you are in a committed but unmarried relationship, it will likely be your partner. If you are unmarried but have adult children, they may be an appropriate choice. If you are unmarried and don't have any children, you'll want to look to parents, siblings, relatives or trusted friends.

The point here is that it's important to consider, in advance, who will be the best person to make health care related decisions for you in the event that you are unable to make them yourself. In addition to your first choice, you'll also want one or more alternates in case your first choice is not available.

In 1996, Congress enacted the Health Insurance Portability and Accountability Act (HIPAA).[3] Several years later, along came The Privacy Rule, which was created to assure that an individual's health information is properly protected, while allowing the flow of health information needed to provide and

---

3 http://www.hhs.gov/ocr/privacy/hipaa/understanding/

promote high quality health care.[4] With limited exceptions, a health care provider may not disclose protected health information without a patient's express written authorization. Failure to follow these rules is a criminal offense and can also result in heavy monetary penalties. Your Health Care Power of Attorney should include a nomination for those persons who will have access to your protected medical information.

Some states have special laws that dictate who will be your health care surrogate if you fail to choose one. If your state does have such a law, do you know who your state has chosen for you? It is always best if *you* make the decision about who will have the authority to make health care decisions for you. Otherwise, the results could be disastrous.

For example, if your state has chosen your spouse to make your health care decisions if you can't, and you are in the process of getting a divorce, he or she may not be your first, or even best, choice.

What if the state's choice is an estranged child you have not spoken to in years? Or, a sibling who lives overseas? Even worse, if you are in an unmarried relationship, your partner will generally be the very last person on the list of authorized persons to make health care decisions for you.

Whether you choose your spouse, your sibling, your parent, your partner or your best friend to be your health care surrogate, part of the estate planning process is ensuring you are taken care of in the event of your incapacity. You'll want to carefully consider who should be a part of your "helper" team to come to your aid when you need them. It starts with naming a person or persons who can speak with your health care

---

4 http://www.hhs.gov/ocr/privacy/hipaa/understanding/summary/

providers and it continues with naming a surrogate who can make health care decisions for you if you cannot.

When selecting your health care surrogate, choose someone you trust—someone you believe will make the same decisions you would make and not substitute their judgment for yours. For example, if you don't believe in blood transfusions and your surrogate does, you have to be comfortable your surrogate will follow your wishes and ignore his or her own. Some people can make decisions inconsistent with their own beliefs, others would find it difficult, and most would find it impossible. Of course, if your surrogate is unaware of your health care and medical beliefs, such as avoiding a blood transfusion, your surrogate may unwittingly act against your wishes.

As a result, your surrogate must know enough about you to know what you would choose. Your surrogate should know your health conditions and your medications, or have access to that information when needed, and your surrogate should especially know if you have strong feelings about any particular treatment. Your chosen surrogate should also have demonstrated care and concern for your welfare and be able to visit you and meet with your health care providers. Your surrogate should also be aware of your religious and moral beliefs.

On February 25, 1990, 26-year-old Terri Schiavo collapsed in her St. Petersburg, Florida, home in full cardiac arrest.[5] She suffered massive brain damage due to lack of oxygen and, after two and a half months in a coma, her diagnosis was elevated to vegetative state. Until 1998, Terri's

_____

5 http://www.terrisfight.org/timeline/

husband, Michael, pursued efforts to rehabilitate her. Then, he petitioned the court for removal of Terri's feeding tube.

Terri had not memorialized her end-of-life wishes in any document. Her parents, Robert and Mary Schindler, disagreed with Michael and wanted Terri maintained on life support. Multiple legal appeals ensued following Michael's request to remove life support. One issue was whether Michael, as Terri's husband, and in the absence of a written direction from Terri, had the right to request termination of life prolonging procedures as a result of Terri's persistent vegetative state.

In 2000, testimony from 18 witnesses was taken regarding Terri's medical condition and her end-of-life wishes. Terri's parents argued that if Terri was conscious, she would not refuse nutrition and hydration, even by artificial means. Michael disagreed and ultimately, Terri's feeding tube was removed. However, the saga continued for several more years.

First, Florida Governor Jeb Bush intervened with a new law called "Terri's Law," and Terri's feeding tube was reinserted.[6] Terri's Law was later overturned and found to be unconstitutional. Do you want the Governor making your end-of-life decisions?

Then, in 2005, the United States Senate attempted to intervene with its own law, and President Bush flew to Washington, D.C. from his vacation in Texas to sign legislation that would keep Terri alive.[7] Do you want the President making your end-of-life decisions?

---

6 http://www.floridalawreview.com/wp-content/uploads/2010/01/Snead_BOOK.pdf

7 https://www.govtrack.us/congress/bills/109/s686/text

On that issue, the U.S. Supreme Court declined to grant the Schindlers' further appeals, effectively ending their judicial options.

After seven years, 14 appeals and numerous motions, petitions and hearings in front of 19 different Florida state court judges, and involvement by the Florida Governor and the President of the United States, Terri Schiavo's feeding tube was permanently removed, and she died under hospice care on March 31, 2005.[8]

Terri's situation attracted a great deal of public attention, primarily because Terri left no instructions and family members disagreed about her wishes. This case brought to light the importance of having written living will instructions regarding end-of-life decisions.

Regardless of your beliefs regarding the removal or retention of life prolonging procedures, it is imperative you memorialize your wishes in writing.

Your living will should also address such things as pain medications or treatments, surgical procedures and the use of a No Code or Do Not Resuscitate order. Every state has different laws regarding end-of-life decisions. A few states have adopted death with dignity provisions allowing individuals the right to choose the time and place of their death.[9] Be sure to consult with an attorney in your state to make sure your health care decisions and your end-of-life wishes are memorialized and are consistent with your state's law.

Health care and end-of-life decisions are an integral part of a comprehensive estate plan designed with your goals in

8 http://www.cnn.com/2005/LAW/03/31/schiavo/

9 http://www.deathwithdignity.org/advocates/national

mind. If your estate planning professional is only focused on what happens to your things after you die, you must voice your concerns to ensure you and your family have all the protection you need.

In October 2009, Anthony Marshall, son of Brooke Astor, socialite and long-reigning matriarch of New York City, was convicted on charges he defrauded his mother and stole tens of millions of dollars from her as she suffered from Alzheimer's in the twilight of her life.[10] A respected philanthropist, Brooke Astor gave away millions of dollars to needy individuals and civic causes in New York City. She died in 2007 at the age of 105. The charges against Anthony arose from a guardianship filed by her grandson, Philip Marshall, who accused his father of looting Mrs. Astor's apartment of art, transferring her properties to his name and keeping her in squalid conditions, confined to a sofa smelling of urine and subsisting on oatmeal and peas.

This story may sound unbelievable and you might imagine that it could never happen to you. Unfortunately, it is not only the very wealthy who are taken advantage of. Every day there are stories about the elderly or infirm who can no longer take care of their own property and finances and are preyed upon by those who pretend to help, but are really just helping themselves to the person's property and money.

Many of us will someday need someone to handle our legal and financial affairs, even if only temporarily, as a result of a mental disability. You could be ill and in the hospital, injured from a car accident or a fall from a horse, or be in

---

10 http://topics.nytimes.com/top/reference/timestopics/people/m/anthony_d_ marshall/index.html

need of long term care and social services as a result of Alzheimer's or dementia.

If you are married, you probably think that you can rely on your spouse. In most cases, you can. However, what happens if your spouse dies first or is already ill or is injured in a common accident? Aside from the fact you never know what will happen, couples often travel together and can be injured together. For that reason, it is important to name others who can act on your behalf if your spouse is unable.

A first step in creating your estate plan is making sure there is no question or issue about who will make legal and financial decisions if your mental capacity is at issue. Your estate planning strategy must include a Durable Financial Power of Attorney—a document that identifies an agent or attorney-in-fact who will act for you with respect to your finances and property, especially in situations where you cannot act for yourself.

It is important your Durable Financial Power of Attorney is specific, clear and comprehensive. You will want your power of attorney to address not only real and personal property, bank accounts, and investment accounts, but also such things as mail, safe deposit boxes, pets, Medicaid planning techniques, Government benefits, taxes, insurance, retirement accounts and trusts.

In some states, if a specific power is not set out in the power of attorney, your agent cannot act for you. Florida, for example, has a comprehensive statute on powers of attorney, and no one will recognize a power of attorney that essentially says "my agent can do everything I can do," because it is too general.[11] Specificity is required for a power of attorney to ensure your wishes will be followed.

Powers of attorney can come in lots of different varieties. They can be durable or non-durable, general or limited, effective immediately or at another date in the future ("springing")—state law will ultimately dictate the flexibility you will have in constructing an instrument to meet your needs.

It's impossible to guarantee you will never be taken advantage of. However, with proper planning and careful thought as to those who are best suited to provide careful and attentive decision making, can help you better protect yourself and your loved ones. If you are unmarried or widowed and don't have children you can trust or your choice of friends is limited, decisions related to your agents and surrogates can be challenging. Even when the decision is a difficult one, it is best for you to make the decision rather than leave the decision to others—unintended family members, or worse, a guardianship judge.

The final step is keeping your disability plan relevant to your current situation. Even if your power of attorney has been drawn up; if it is more than a few years old or there has been a change in the law or it still identifies your agent daughter by her maiden name, your bank or other financial institution may not honor it.

If you have not reviewed your power of attorney recently, you may find that it names someone you no longer trust. If that is the case, do not hesitate to see an attorney to revise your power of attorney to name a new agent and successors.

---

11 http://www.leg.state.fl.us/Statutes/index.cfm?App_mode=Display_ Statute&Search_String=&URL=0700-0799/0709/0709PARTIIContentsIndex.html

You never know when an accident or illness will strike, and the time to find out your plan doesn't work isn't when you need it most.

CHAPTER 3

Doesn't the Government Pay for Long Term Care?

If you've planned for mental disability, then you're ahead of the game.

But don't stop there.

Planning for long term care requires a different planning and thought process. Planning for long term care means considering all the options for what would happen if you or a loved one needs to spend an extended period of time in a nursing home or needs to move permanently from home to a long term care facility—either assisted living or nursing home.

Your best defense against the rising cost of long term care is insurance. Long term care insurance can help defray the cost of in-home care, assisted living care and nursing home care. The mistake most people make is to believe they will never need long term care or if they do, their family will be in a position to provide care at home. Frequently, people say, "I'll never go into a nursing home." Never say, "Never." Visit a nursing home and ask each one of those people whether they ever planned to live in a nursing home. The answer will certainly be a resounding, "No."

Long term care insurance is like every other kind of insurance—you can't get it when you need it. You need to get it when you are relatively young, insurable and the premiums are less expensive. That way, when you need it, you'll have it. What if you never need it? Then, congratulations! You beat the odds. No one ever hopes to need their auto, homeowner's or life insurance either, but they sure are nice to have when you do.

Work with an insurance professional who has expertise in long term care insurance. There are lots of choices to make and lots of consequences for making the wrong choices. You'll have to decide on the daily rate, a cost of living adjust-ment rider, length of time the policy will pay, and death benefit options, just to name a few. There are new products coming onto the market every day, so find a professional who knows and understands how to help you find the best policy.

If you don't have long term care insurance and you need long term care, there are some common payment sources. Medicare will pay for short term nursing home or rehabilitative care, but not long term care. A Medicare supplement can help defray some of the expenses (most commonly, the co-pay) of a short term nursing home or rehab stay, but again, not for the long term. If you are a veteran and you meet certain service requirements, you may be entitled to assistance under the pension program known as Aid & Attendance. You don't have to be a retired veteran to qualify, but you do have to meet the prescribed service requirement, be honorably discharged and qualify under income and asset limitations. Personal resources and/or family resources may be another option for defraying the cost of long term care. If your resources are limited and you've done proper planning, then Medicaid may provide long term care assistance. Currently, Medicaid is the ONLY government source for long term care available today.

Each state's Medicaid program is different. Although Medicaid is a federal program, the states have the flexibility to implement the program in different ways. As a result, don't rely on information from friends or relatives who live in a different state—likely, the rules and the benefits are not the same.

Your best source of information for Medicaid planning is a qualified elder law attorney. In Florida, look for someone who is board certified in elder law. In states that don't have a board certification program, the National Academy of Elder Law Attorneys (NAELA) offers a certification program for Certified Elder Law Attorney (CELA).[12] Certification programs are intended to award those attorneys whose education and experience meet high standards and indicate a high level of dedication to the practice area. Beware of sales people who hold themselves out as Medicaid planning professionals—if they aren't a qualified elder law attorney, get a second opinion before relying on their advice.

Planning for long term care generally involves a comprehensive review of assets—their nature, value and ownership. Planning options may depend on whether you are a single or married person. Many programs are available only for nursing home care, but some states have in-home care or assisted living programs. In some cases, there may be a waiting list in order to qualify for benefits under one or more programs.

A common planning scenario might be an older single woman whose has assets of approximately $200,000. She can afford to pay for long term care for a period of time, but

---

12 http://www.naela.org/

not more than a couple of years. Does she have to spend all of her money before she can qualify for Medicaid to provide assistance with her long term care? She doesn't have to, but the uninformed may assume that is the only option-spend it all, then apply when there is no money left. Instead, she can implement some planning strategies that may provide a different solution. She can prepay her burial and funeral, so long as she isn't able to access the cash-generally accomplished with an irrevocable rider. In addition, she can establish a burial account to help defray expenses that have not been prepaid. In Florida, her homestead property and a car would also be considered exempt assets. Other planning options might include income producing real property, a personal service contract, or a pooled trust. Each state has established rules regarding exempt assets and income limitations. The point is that there are planning options that should be considered before making a decision about long term care. These options will vary depending on the state of residence and sometimes it makes sense to relocate to a state with better benefits.

This area of the law is very complex and touches numerous other areas of the law. It is not for do-it-yourselfers as a negative outcome could have a catastrophic result for a loved one requiring long term care. Consult with a qualified professional for the best results.

CHAPTER FOUR

Where There's a Will, There's a Way... Or Is There?

So far, we've explored why planning is important, planning for mental disability, and planning for long-term care.

The final frontier is planning for what happens when you die.

A Last Will and Testament (Last Will or Will) sets forth your wishes regarding the distribution of your assets, the payment of your debts at the time of death and the nomination of guardians for minor children—it has no other purpose. Additionally, it will name the person or persons who will be responsible for the administration of your estate—they become your personal representative or executor. For minor children, the person you select as their guardian will be responsible for their care in your absence. Your Last Will only controls the assets you own in your *individual* name and guarantees probate, a process most people believe they want to avoid.

This chapter could also be titled "Why Estate Plans Don't Work."

Most people assume if they have a Last Will it will address all of the issues that could arise at the time of death. Nothing could be further from the truth.

The fact is, many Wills are completely irrelevant at the time someone dies. The reason—the assets of the decedent were not owned consistent with the instructions set forth in the Will.

Here's an example of a "typical" nuclear family—a husband, a wife, and two children.

How do most married individuals own their property? As joint owners, of course.

As a nation, we are raised to believe that the proper way for a husband and wife to own their property is as joint tenants with rights of survivorship or as tenants by the entirety (a state law concept of ownership for husbands and wives). The intention is if one spouse dies, the other spouse will inherit the property.

This may appear all well and good on its face and it is a plan referred to as an "I love you" plan. Here's an example: The husband dies, the wife now owns everything—no probate, no problem. Or is there? What happens if the wife re-marries at some point in the future? What happens if she and her new husband, (I'll call him Biff the Tennis Pro) begin to own their property jointly? What happens if the wife dies and Biff survives? What happens if she and Biff should divorce?

The scenario above is very common—it happens every single day. No one gets hurt until someone dies or gets a divorce. If the wife and Biff own their property jointly and the wife dies—Biff owns everything! Who is rolling over in their grave now? What is Biff's obligation to provide for the two children of the first marriage? Absolutely none. If the wife and Biff get divorced, jointly owned property is generally divided equally, leaving the children from the first marriage with potentially less than their parents intended.

Could this situation have been avoided? Definitely, but it requires education and planning.

Instead of owning all of their property jointly, assets could be divided equally between the husband and wife. Then when the first spouse dies, the instructions in their Last Will (or trust) sets forth what happens next. In a perfect world, there will be a testamentary trust created for the benefit of the surviving spouse. This trust can be constructed to provide asset protection, remarriage protection and even long term care asset protection. In addition, the assets can be protected for the children or other intended beneficiaries. If the spouse needs help with the management of the trust assets, a trustee other than the spouse can be appointed for that purpose.

Often, after the death of the first spouse, the surviving spouse becomes concerned about what might happen in the future if they should become disabled. Sadly, a common solution is to visit the neighborhood bank branch to seek advice. Generally, the result is the bank representative will advise that the best solution is to put one (or more) of the children's names on the account. Sadly, this small act could have disastrous results.

It solves one problem—access to the account in case the parent needs assistance with bill paying—but it creates the potential for so many more problems. Putting a child's name on an account is the same as giving the child the right to own that account. As a result, when the parent dies, the account owner child is now the sole owner of the account with no obligation to share those assets with any other person, e.g. the other children.

This is true regardless of what the Last Will says!

Further, in the event the account owner child should get divorced or sued while the parent is still living, the parent's assets could become subject to confiscation by the creditor (or predator). This is not something that happens only in the movies—it happens every single day with disastrous results.

This same result also occurs when a parent puts their child's name on a piece of real property. Only in this case, adding the child's name results in a completed gift.

Many people are unaware of the consequences of such a gift. The IRS says that you can give away $14,000 per year (the annual gift exclusion) to as many people as you'd like.[13] If you stay at or under $14,000 there is no obligation to report the gift to the IRS (Form 709). If the gift exceeds $14,000, then a timely filed gift tax return will be required. Many gifts go unreported and the IRS is starting to crack down.

Sometimes clients ask how the IRS will ever discover an unreported gift. The answer falls into the same category as failure to file your annual income tax return. The law requires you to report your income. The law also requires you to report gifts made over the annual exclusion amount of $14,000. The IRS recognizes that millions of dollars of unreported gifts are made annually and they are taking steps to identify people who are violating the law. Checking the public records

13 http://www.irs.gov/Businesses/Small-Businesses-&-Self-Employed/
Frequently-Asked-Questions-on-Gift-Taxes

for recorded deeds is just one way the IRS is discovering reporting violations.

If IRS reporting doesn't concern you because you'll never have enough assets to incur a future gift or estate tax, gifts can also have serious consequences for long-term care planning. Most states impose a penalty for gifts made in the five years prior to making an application for Medicaid. Often gifts are made inadvertently or on the advice of a well-meaning person who doesn't grasp the gravity of the gift process for Medicaid applicants. Seek professional guidance before making gifts of any kind—both for estate planning and long-term care planning concerns.

In addition to the potential gift issue, once a child's name is added to an asset, the potential for confiscation by a creditor is real. In the case of a parent's home, it may also have homestead consequences, both for taxation and creditor protection depending on your state. And, gifts are generally permanent. You can't change your mind and later demand a return of the gift.

Another potential problem with adding a child's name to a property (or even making an outright gift) is a capital gains tax concern.

A transfer of assets carries with it a transfer of the tax basis. For example, if you paid $10,000 for an asset, that's your tax basis.[14] If the asset grows in value to $50,000 and you give it away, you've also given away the $10,000 tax basis. If the gift recipient now sells the asset, they will have the obligation to report a $40,000 gain and pay the appropriate capital

---

14 http://www.irs.gov/Businesses/Small-Businesses-&-Self-Employed/
Frequently-Asked-Questions-on-Gift-Taxes

gains tax. If an asset is, instead, transferred at death, the tax basis is increased to the value of the property at the date of death. If the date of death value is $50,000 that becomes the new tax basis and the capital gain can be avoided.

The bottom line is a Last Will is an important and effective estate planning tool, but only if you understand its interaction with asset ownership and beneficiary designations.

One way to avoid the problems with adding another person's name, either as a gift or for the sake of convenience, is to nominate that same person as your agent in a valid power of attorney. A power of attorney will allow your nominated agent to act on your behalf but without any of the gift, transfer or potential creditor issues.

Powers of attorney are effective during your lifetime, and a Will takes effect at the time of your death.

In both cases, the person(s) you choose to carry out these important roles should be someone you trust implicitly. Don't choose your eldest child or the child who expects to be chosen because they live closest. In some cases, it may not be wise to choose your children at all. Some people don't have children and as a result will have to rely on other family members, friends or professionals.

Your agent during your lifetime will have the responsibility for paying your bills, filing your taxes and handling all of your important legal and financial transactions. If you need nursing home care they will be responsible for making sure you are capable of meeting the financial obligations. They won't be expected to use their own resources, but to maximize the use of yours including applying for any government benefits you are entitled to.

Your personal representative, executor, or successor trustee will be responsible for the administration of your estate at the time of death. They will need to identify, gather and value your assets, pay your creditors, and make the proper distributions according to your wishes as laid out in your Last Will or trust.

If you believe your children or your heirs will all get along and work everything out as you desire, it doesn't always happen that way!

Petty childhood grievances and other family baggage tend to surface when one or both parents are ill or have died. When families fight, lawyers win—a lawsuit among family members can be costly, both emotionally and financially. In addition, families rarely reconcile after litigation ensues. Your goal should be to consider all the possible outcomes related to your estate plan. Your attorney should be able to help you think of things that you might not. A smooth, efficient administration, either during disability or death, is necessary to maintain family harmony.

When you are ready to create your estate plan, find an experienced attorney who will educate and counsel you so your plan works the way you want. Don't attempt to use an online Will creation service, a form from an office supply store or the least expensive attorney you can find. This aspect of your life is just too important.

You have the power to create the plan you want, for yourself and your loved ones. If you fail to plan, your state has a plan for you. If you own your assets inconsistent with your plan, it is doomed to fail. Remember, if you fail to plan, you have planned to fail.

CHAPTER FIVE

Can You Trust Your Family?

Love all, trust a few.

~ Shakespeare

A Living Trust is an estate planning directive that allows you to control your assets while you are alive and well, plan for yourself and your loved ones in the event of your mental disability and then give what you have, to whom you want, when you want, the way you want.

Trusts are essentially three-party contracts where you get to be all three parties while you are alive and well. You are the trustmaker (grantor/settler/trustor), the trustee (the person responsible for the daily investment, administration and distribution of trust assets) and the beneficiary during your lifetime. At the end of your lifetime, your trust assets will avoid probate, can save estate taxes and can continue to benefit your family for generations to come.

The benefits of having a fully funded trust and leaving your inheritance in trust for your spouse, children or other heirs are numerous. With a trust, you can:

1. Provide continuity in the handling of your affairs by more efficiently transferring your property to your loved ones.

2. Provide comfort to your loved ones during their period of grief and spare them unnecessary emotional or financial hardship should you become incapacitated and at the time of your death.

3. Allow your family to avoid probate on your death, and avoid court guardianship proceedings on your disability, for all assets owned or controlled by your trust.

4. Provide remarriage protection for your spouse and children should your surviving spouse choose to remarry after your death—it can help assure that your estate passes to your children and not to the new spouse.

5. Ensure that your trust easily moves with you from state to state.

6. Create trusts for minor children and children who are disabled that are free from the supervision of the probate court. A special needs trust will also ensure no loss of government benefits.

7. Retain control over your minor child's inheritance, rather than allowing the inheritance to get into the hands of your ex-spouse or the guardianship court. In a guardianship, the court is required to distribute all funds directly to the child at age 18, a result you may not want.

8. Create trusts for adult children for the purpose of providing them with divorce protection, creditor

protection and if necessary, protection from themselves if they have a drug, alcohol, chemical dependency disorder, a gambling addiction or they are incarcerated. Trusts can also protect adult children from carelessly spending their inheritance—an ailment commonly known as "affluenza."

9. Protect an unmarried partner at the time of your death to ensure assets are protected for their benefit while allowing you to direct the distribution of remaining trust assets at the death of your partner.

10. Create trusts for the benefit of pets to ensure they receive lifetime care before assets are distributed to other beneficiaries, including charities and family members.

11. Guarantee the "stretch out" of your IRA benefits and the maximization of benefits to the family while minimizing income tax consequences.

12. Help assure your family's privacy following your disability and death.

13. Protect your children's inheritance from a former spouse or step-parent if you should you die first.

14. Achieve your death tax objectives by reducing or avoiding estate tax.

15. Reduce after-death administrative expenses.

16. Pass assets more quickly to your loved ones upon your death, avoiding some of the delays, hassles, and paperwork involved in the probate process.

17. Provide peace of mind for yourself now and for your family later.

As you can see, a Living Trust based plan has many benefits.

The first step in creating a Living Trust plan that "works" is selecting the right attorney, educating yourself about your options, engaging in a comprehensive design meeting and then understanding the plan you've created before you sign it. But you're not done there. Funding or asset integration is an important part of your Living Trust plan. It means you need to re-title assets into the name of your trust and/or rename beneficiary designations on life insurance, retirement plans and annuities so they all point to the instructions in your trust. Without this step, your plan is nothing more than a stack of papers and all your hard work may have been futile. However, without assistance and some guidance, this task can be overwhelming. Make sure your legal counselor provides assistance to make sure this step is done right.

Here's an example. Bob and Mary Smith create a Living Trust based plan with their trusted legal counsel. This plan allows Bob and Mary to control their assets during their lifetime. Although assets are re-titled to the name of their respective trusts, they are still in total control. In addition, their trust contains instructions about what should happen if either of them becomes mentally disabled during their lifetime. The trust appoints their successor or disability trustees so someone can take over the day-to-day management of their assets if they are no longer able. Then, when either Bob or Mary dies, their trust contains instructions for a multi-fold purpose. First, to make sure they take advantage of the estate tax laws then in effect. These instructions will allow them to avoid any potential estate tax on the death of the first spouse. A second purpose is asset protection for the surviving spouse. The trust instructions can provide for a distribution standard that will allow for maximum access to the assets by the surviving spouse, but still provide protection from creditors (bankruptcy, litigation, remarriage/divorce). In addition, if the surviving spouse needs guidance from a co-trustee, this information can be included as well. Here too, is where the instructions intended to provide remarriage protection are also included. After both Bob and Mary have died, the trust sets forth instructions for continuing trusts for the benefit of their children and grandchildren. These lifetime protective trusts ensure the assets Bob and Mary leave for their family stay with their family.

Sounds great, right? Yes, but this plan only works if Bob and Mary actually re-title their assets so the trust instructions are relevant. Far too often, couples create a well-designed plan and then continue life as usual. Most often, they continue to own their assets jointly. As a result, when the first spouse dies, everything passes directly to the surviving spouse. As a result, there's no estate tax protection, no asset protection, no remarriage protection and no instructions for assistance in the event the survivor needs help. This happens far too often. Here, an unfunded trust was absolutely not worth the paper it was written on.

Imagine this scenario. A married person dies with a $200,000 life insurance policy. The policy names the surviving spouse as the beneficiary. There are five children that require raising and educating. However, the surviving spouse has a creditor from a failed business transaction in the exact same amount, $200,000. Does the creditor care that the survivor needs to raise these five children? No! The only thing the creditor cares about is getting paid and here's the perfect opportunity. This situation could have turned out very differently if those proceeds had instead been paid to a trust for the benefit of the surviving spouse and children.

Trusts are often misunderstood and some people believe them to be too complex. However, just the opposite is true. A well drafted trust, fully funded with the trustmaker's assets or named as beneficiary of life insurance and retirement plans, can provide significant opportunities and avoid future problems.

Trusts come in many varieties—revocable living trusts, irrevocable trusts, charitable trusts, trust for business purposes, trusts for gift or estate tax purposes, trusts for long term care asset protection planning purposes.

Yes, it can all become overwhelming!

Most advanced planning techniques are beyond the scope of this book. Be sure to consult with your estate planning professional for guidance on advanced planning trust techniques and get all the education and information you need before making a decision.

CHAPTER SIX

What if I Have Unique Planning Concerns?

Not every planning situation is going to be easy. Often families have unique planning concerns that require unique planning solutions. This chapter addresses a few of the situations that might arise.

Unmarried Partners and Same Sex Couples

Unmarried partners, either same sex or opposite sex, provide interesting planning opportunities, along with some challenges. You can't just plug in what you know about planning for married couples or planning for single individuals. The rules are definitely different for couples who are in a committed but unmarried relationship.

Unmarried couples have a lot of the same concerns as married couples but very few of the protections afforded married couples under the law. In fact, there are more than 1,100 state and federal rights a person gains when they get married that are not available to singles.[15] Without proper planning,

---

15 http://www.hrc.org/resources/entry/an-overview-of-federal-rights-and-protections-granted-to-married-couples

unmarried couples do not have the ability to make legal, financial or health care decisions on behalf of their partner. It is essential to prepare the appropriate legal directives—Durable Financial Powers of Attorney, Health Care Powers of Attorney and Living Wills. In addition, trust planning may be appropriate so each partner has the ability to protect the other (including other loved ones) in the event of a mental disability and at death.

Unmarried couples can't take advantage of unlimited lifetime and death gifting opportunities. As a result, unmarried partners must carefully monitor gifting between themselves to avoid gift tax reporting consequences and unintentionally using their lifetime gift exclusion. Simply owning an asset jointly can create an unexpected or unintended gift.

State laws favor the married status of couples. Unmarried couples have no rights under family law statutes and are rarely a preference under probate or health care statutes. Estate and gift tax laws are also unfavorable for unmarried partners. In a few instances, there may be tax advantages for the succession of business interests but those opportunities are limited.

An unmarried partner has no rights in the property of a deceased partner unless created by a Last Will or Living Trust or in the form of ownership such as joint tenants with rights of survivorship. Retirement plan laws don't protect unmarried couples. The Social Security system and its laws provide no protection for the surviving partner in the event of death. If one partner gives up their career and no longer pays into Social Security, they may also be giving up rights related to disability and retirement.

We live in an ever changing legal environment. Today, some states recognize same sex marriage. Federal laws now treat same sex marriages in the same way they treat heterosexual marriages. Complications can arise, however, because not all states recognize same sex marriage and as a result, state laws still may not provide a married same sex couple with any protection. Planning for unmarried couples and same sex partners requires attention to many different areas of the law. Be sure to consult with a qualified professional before undertaking planning on your own.

Two resources for your further review include *Loving Without a License—An Estate Planning Survival Guide for Unmarried Couples and Same Sex Partners,* by this author along with Candace Pollock[16] and *Whether to Wed* by Scott Squillace—both are available on Amazon.com.

Special Family Members

Many families who have loved ones with special needs rely on SSI, Medicaid or other needs-based government benefits to provide food, shelter and basic medical care. The assistance available could be dependent upon the state where you live. If you are a family with a special person, you undoubtedly know that while these state and federal public benefits are very valuable, more is needed for your special person to fully enjoy life.

Ensuring your special person is well provided for without jeopardizing benefits can seem impossible. Unfortunately,

---

16 *Loving Without a License—An Estate Planning Survival Guide for Unmarried Partners and Same Sex* Couples, Peggy R. Hoyt and Candace Pollock, LegacyPlanningPartners.org.

most "plans" fail either because families try to cut corners and do it themselves or they don't work with someone who has expertise in this area of the law.

Some families are actually advised to disinherit their special family member—the very person who needs the help most!

This "solution" simply does not allow you to ensure that your special person is protected if you become incapacitated and when you die. Some families procrastinate, believing that today or even tomorrow is not the day they will be faced with a crisis—what is known as the "not me, not now" syndrome. The preferable rule is, "It's never too early to plan, because you never know when it's going to be too late."

Some families believe they can rely on the kindness of other family members to provide financially for a disabled special person. This is reflected in beneficiary designations on retirement plans and insurance policies that name other family member with the idea that the named individual will provide for the special person.

The reality is, you can't control what other family members will do with the money, and they will have no legal obligation to provide for the special person. In addition, unexpected occurrences for that other person, such as divorce, creditor issues, incapacity, and death can completely change the outcome you've intended. Rather than rely on others to provide and plan for your special person after you're gone, get your own good advice, do your own planning, and consider your best possible solution—a properly drafted Special Needs Trust.

In one tragic situation, a well-meaning parent named a grandparent as the beneficiary for a life insurance policy, fully expecting the grandparent to provide for the needs of the special child. Instead, when the parent died unexpectedly, the grandparent accepted the life insurance proceeds but provided nothing for the benefit of the child. This not-so-uncommon situation could have been easily avoided with a Special Needs Trust.

The primary purpose of a Special Needs Trust is to maintain your special person's eligibility for needs-based state and federal benefits while preserving adequate funds for additional needs not provided by government programs. Funds held by a Special Needs Trust do not count toward resource eligibility requirements, so the Special Needs Trust can pay for items not provided by public benefits without jeopardizing your special person's eligibility for those benefits. That is, the Special Needs Trust can provide funds to enhance your special person's life. Items the Special Needs Trust can provide include medications, medical equipment and therapies; educational and vocational programs; transportation; hobbies, sports, recreation and entertainment; travel for medical or recreational purposes; and possibly a personal assistant or care manager; just to name a few.

A Special Needs Trust provides a benefit for other family members as well. Without a Special Needs Trust, your special person may receive a gift or an inheritance outright from someone who doesn't understand that the receipt of a gift or inheritance could jeopardize continued eligibility for the benefits. With a Special Needs Trust, family members and friends can make lifetime or testamentary gifts directly to the trust without causing a loss of benefits.

With a Special Needs Trust, you can accomplish the following:

- Preserve government benefits
- Protect the funds from creditors and divorce
- Choose who will serve as trustee and as advisors
- Provide clear instructions with a helpful structure
- You can still call upon your family members to assist in ways that they can be most helpful

By doing so, you lessen the burden on all family members and yet promote a loving, involved and supportive relationship among them. A Special Needs Trust is one of the most valuable gifts you can give your special person.

For more information, read *Special People, Special Planning—Creating a Safe Legal Haven for Families with Special Needs*[17], by this author along with Candace Pollock and available at Amazon.com.

Pets are Family Too!

If you are a pet lover, than you know that pets are family too!

Many people have no two-legged children, just the kind with four legs and fur coats! Including your pets as part of your estate plan should be as natural as planning for minor children who require special care and attention. Pets can't take care of themselves so you have to give special consideration to their needs in the event of your disability and at your death.

---

17 *Special People, Special Planning—Creating a Safe Legal Haven for Families with Special Needs,* Peggy R. Hoyt and Candace Pollock, LegacyPlanningPartners.org.

Annabelle's Story is unfortunately a more common occurrence than most pet lovers would want to believe.

Annabelle's Story

My name is Annabelle, and I'm lonely and scared. Yesterday morning, my friend and I went for our usual run. Then she fed me, filled my water bowl, and brushed me before going off to work. Now it's dark again . . . for the second time.

My friend is usually home before dark, and I'm always so glad to see her. She hugs me and takes good care of me. She feeds me again and we play in the backyard or take a walk before going to bed.

I'm so hungry, and all my water is gone. Why isn't my friend home?! Does anyone know I'm here . . . alone? I've been barking but nobody has come, and now I'm just too tired to bark anymore. I'm scared. What's going to happen to me?

Wait, I hear someone at the door, yippee . . . but it's not my friend—I don't know who these people are. They're carrying a cage and coming towards me. Where are they taking me? Oh why did my friend leave me?!

What happened to Annabelle's friend?

The possibilities are limited only by your imagination. She may have been seriously injured in an auto accident or, worse yet, she may have died. She may have been the victim of a violent crime or stricken with a sudden, serious illness. It's hard to believe that any of these things will happen to us, but the truth is that today could be your turn to be that "someone else" these things usually happen to.

Despite their short life expectancy, your pet may very well outlive you, or you may become disabled. If you don't come home today, would someone you trust:

- Remember your pet and know how to gain access to your home?

- Know your pet's feeding schedule and other routines?

- Know how to find and administer your pet's medication?

- Be willing to take your pet home or find a new permanent loving home?

- Have the time and financial resources to care for your pet?

Planning for the care of your pet will give you peace of mind in knowing that your pet will receive love and proper care in the event of your disability and at your death. Without planning, your pet may be left to the mercy of those who have little or no affection for your pet. How would you feel if the people you trusted opened the door and released your dogs to the world, expecting them to fend for themselves or find a new home?

Think it can't happen? It can, and Annabelle's story is actually a true story!

If you do nothing else, talk to the person or persons you believe will care for your pets should something happen to you, and make sure they are willing and have the financial resources to care for your pet. Make sure they know how to get into your home and how to access information about the care of your pets.

If you want to do more, a Pet Trust is your best planning solution. It will ensure the right people are appointed to care for your pet, provide sufficient funds for that care and appoint a trustee to make sure your instructions are carried out.

With a Pet Trust, you

- Choose your pet's future caregiver
- Provide financially for the care of your pet
- Provide information about your pet that only you may know
- Provide directions for such things as health care, exercise and recreation, diet and
- nutrition, and end-of-life decisions
- Ensure remaining funds to go to a charity, friend or family member

Keep in mind that unwritten agreements with family or friends often go awry, because

- Emotions, personal circumstances and who you trust can change.
- Money left outright may go not for the care of your pet, but to possible
- creditors, a former spouse or any other unforeseen situation.

Finally, consider developing a relationship with a reliable pet sitter. Make your choice before an emergency occurs. Even if you have family nearby, they will appreciate having assistance with your pet while they are caring or grieving for you. Having someone who knows your pet and your routine will help greatly when making the transition to your substitute pet caregiver.

Animal Care Trust can provide trustee services for you and your pet. It's the only trustee program solely dedicated to the needs of pet owners and their pets. Animal Care Trust can provide the investment and administrative oversight necessary to ensure your pets are taken care of for the rest of their lives. For more information, visit AnimalCareTrust.com.

For more information about planning for your pet, read *All My Children Wear Fur Coats—How to Leave a Legacy for Your Pet*[18], available at Amazon.com.

---

18 *All My Children Wear Fur Coats—How to Leave a Legacy for your Pet*, Peggy R. Hoyt, LegacyForYourPet.com.

CHAPTER SEVEN

Are Taxes a Big Concern?

"I'm proud to be paying taxes in the United States. The only thing is—I could be just as proud for half the money."

~ *Arthur Godfrey*

There are three main categories of taxes that may be triggered when dealing with a Last Will, a Living Trust and assets transferred during lifetime or at death. These categories are:

- Income taxes, which includes taxes on earned income, investment income and capital gains (or losses)

- Gift taxes

- Estate taxes, called inheritance taxes or estate transfer taxes in some states, and can include generation-skipping taxes

Whether you or your estate are subject to one or all areas of these taxes depends on many factors such as your income tax bracket, whether you are married or single (including unmarried couples), whether you live in a community or separate property state, your net worth at your death, whether your state taxes transfers of assets at death in addition to the federal estate taxes that might be due, and other consider-ations such as how trust provisions are drafted, how assets are titled and ultimately, how your estate will be administered.

Tax planning can be complex and challenging. The rules change frequently and courts give conflicting interpretations of the rules. Some advisors focus their practice on tax planning and, indeed, some advisors and their clients can let the tax tail wag the estate planning dog. Essentially what that means is your estate plan shouldn't be all about taxes—they are only one consideration in creating your overall plan.

If you have a general understanding of the three main categories of taxes, you will be in a better position to under-stand the recommendations your advisors might offer and then make good decisions about how you want to structure your estate plan. Failure to consider the tax consequences of gifts you make during your lifetime and at death, acquisitions or disposal of assets and other factors can cause you or your survivors to pay more taxes than necessary. Smart planning within the rules will allow you to utilize more assets during your lifetime and increase the value of assets for your loved ones at your death.

As mentioned, tax rules change regularly and the interpretations of these rules are dynamic. So it's important to regularly update your plan to make sure it stays current with your goals, circumstances, tax laws and your net worth. Only a plan kept current will allow you to take advantage of planning opportunities and avoid dangers for yourself and your loved ones.

Income Taxes

Investment assets can be invested for growth and/or income. Assets sold at a gain or loss will be subject to income tax rules regarding the gain or loss. If a trust is involved, the income tax might be attributable to the trustmaker or to the trust itself, depending on the terms of the trust. The general rule is that "grantor trusts," where the trustmaker is the trustee, are taxed to the trustmaker at his or her individual tax rates.[19]

If the trustmaker has given up sufficient control over the trust, as in the case of an irrevocable trust, the income is generally taxed to the trust as a separate entity. Income taxed at trust tax rates often results in higher taxes than if taxed at individual tax rates. However, there may be compelling reasons why a person might opt to assume higher tax rates under a trust rather than the lower individual rates. These reasons generally relate to increased protections from other categories of taxes, increased creditor protections or other desired planning goals.

An often overlooked area of taxes is the capital gains tax. There are two considerations—one has to do with lifetime gifts and the other with gifts made at the time of death. A gift made during lifetime will transfer the donor's original basis (the price they paid for the gifted item). As a result, if you paid $1,000 for a painting and gifted it during your lifetime when it is worth $5,000, the individual receiving the gift has your original $1,000 basis and if they sell the painting for $5,000, they will have to pay capital gains tax on $4,000. If that same painting, however, were given at death, the recipient would receive what's called a "step up in basis." The receiver of the gift gets

---

19 http://www.irs.gov/instructions/i1041/ch01.html#d0e744

an increase in basis to the fair market value on the date of your death. So the same painting received at death has a $5,000 basis and if sold for that same amount, the recipient will incur no capital gains tax at all. As you can see, the timing of gifts can be crucial to minimizing exposure to capital gains tax, especially on appreciated assets.[20]

Gift Taxes

Under current gift tax rules, annual gifts of up to $14,000 (current figure) per person per year are excluded from your lifetime gift tax limit—currently $5,340,000 (adjusted annually for inflation). This means you may give as many gifts of $14,000 or less each year to as many individuals as you desire without incurring a gift tax obligation or an obligation to file a gift tax return. Married individuals can give unlimited gifts to each other and may join together and give up to $28,000 per year to others for the purposes of making annual exclusion gifts (this is called "gift splitting"). Certain other gifts may be made without using the $14,000 annual exclusion amount, but you should discuss those with your tax professional to make sure they are done correctly.[21]

Annual gifts are one strategy to transfer assets from someone who has assets over the estate tax applicable exclusion amount or simply for the purpose of making lifetime gifts that can be enjoyed while the gift-giver is still alive and well. Consider that the estate tax applicable exclusion amount is adjusted annually for inflation and can also be changed by Congress, so it is important to review your plan periodically.

20 http://www.irs.gov/uac/Ten-Important-Facts-About-Capital-Gains-and-Losses

21 http://www.irs.gov/Businesses/Small-Businesses-&-Self-Employed/ Frequently-Asked-Questions-on-Gift-Taxes

If you are concerned about gift taxes, it is important to coordinate your lifetime gifts with your probable distributions (gifts) at your death to avoid unnecessary taxes. If you anticipate having taxable gifts, you should work with your professional advisors to decide how to minimize your tax exposure.

Gifts made for the purpose of reducing a person's estate for Medicaid or VA planning purposes may be subject to reporting for IRS purposes. However, generally in the Medicaid and VA arena we aren't concerned about using a person's lifetime exemption. Be careful here—the rules related to Medicaid gifts are not the same as the rules for gifts for IRS purposes. A $14,000 gift from a Medicaid perspective may carry an eligibility penalty while the same gift from an IRS perspective is not taxable or reportable.

Estate Taxes

The obligation to pay estate taxes depends on the size of your estate. Currently, if an estate is less than $5,340,000 and death occurs in 2014, your estate will not have any liability for federal estate taxes.[22] This can be a tricky area, however, for a number of reasons. First, people are not always clear about what is included in their taxable estate. Second, the estate tax exemption amount can change. Third, even though there may not be a federal tax, some states have lower estate tax limits and there may be a state estate tax.

Generally, everything you own, everything you control and everything with your name on it gets included for estate tax purposes. This means that your jointly held property (at

22 http://www.irs.gov/Businesses/Small-Businesses-&-Self-Employed/Estate-and-Gift-Taxes

least a portion of it), everything you own individually, all your life insurance policies (not just the cash value but the death benefit value), your retirement plans including your IRA, 401k, deferred compensation, and so forth are included in your taxable estate.

The "estate tax applicable exclusion" amount, also known as the "estate tax exemption" amount, is the amount each person can leave free of estate taxes at death. As mentioned, it is currently $5,340,000 but that amount surely can and will change in the future. Right now, it is adjusted annually for inflation.

Estate taxes are essentially a voluntary tax in the sense that you can "volunteer" to pay them by failing to adequately plan. With proper planning, the estate taxes due on your death can be minimized or avoided. However, avoiding payment of unnecessary taxes requires education and then action. Seek out the advice of a qualified tax or legal professional to assist you in structuring your estate in a way that will minimize the estate tax effects on your estate and provide the maximum inheritance to your loved ones.

Generation skipping taxes are another level of tax that may be incurred when the trustmaker elects to "skip" a generation with regard to gifting.[23] To skip a generation doesn't mean your children won't benefit from your assets, only that they won't be responsible for the payment of any associated estate tax. These estate taxes are deferred to future generations and must be paid upon distribution to the subsequent generations. Currently the generation skipping tax is unified with the estate tax and is currently at $5,340,000. Again, that

23 http://www.irs.gov/uac/Form-709,-United-States-Gift-%28and-Generation-Skipping-Transfer%29-Tax-Return

number changes regularly. Planning for generation skipping taxes is a complex area of the law, and consultation with your legal advisor and tax professional is highly recommended.

Tax law changes are an example of why estate plans must be updated. Although legal and financial advisors can create directives and build plans to withstand many of the anticipated changes in the law, your best interests are served if your estate plan is subjected to professional scrutiny from time to time.

It's Not Just About Taxes

Minimizing income, gift and estate taxes is an admirable goal, but it shouldn't be the only reason you do planning. Estate planning can accomplish many goals including the protection of yourself and your loved ones. Sometimes tax strategies create more complexity than families are prepared to deal with. So weigh the costs and benefits and make a decision that works for you.

Work with a professional who can listen to all of your goals and help you design a plan that best meets the needs of you and your family, while accomplishing your lifetime gift and estate tax goals.

CHAPTER TEN

What Should I do When Someone Dies?

"Leave your kids enough money so they would feel they can do anything, but not so much that they could do nothing."

~ Warren Buffett

Prudent planning is all about making sure you have a plan that works the way you wish, so you may have peace of mind now, and your family may have peace of mind when you are gone. After all, once you're gone, there is no fixing a broken plan.

Whether you die with just a Last Will or with a Living Trust, there will be work to be done after your death.

While most people are anxious to avoid probate and attempt to use trusts to avoid the probate process, trusts are often unfunded, meaning there are few, if any, assets titled in the name of the trust. In that case, some form of probate is inevitable. Of course, if the only goal is to avoid probate, then there may be possible other disastrous results for the family.

Adding a child's name to an asset or a financial account may be one way to avoid probate but could have gift, Medicaid planning and asset protection implications. If the gift exceeds the annual exclusion of $14,000, a gift tax return will be required. If the child's name is added in the five year period preceding an application for Medicaid, there could be an uncompensated transfer penalty. If a child has a catastrophic creditor event or divorce, the asset could become entangled in a lawsuit. Each of these possibilities is real so adding a child's name to anything should only be done in consultation with the oversight of a legal professional.

A Last Will becomes effective upon death and controls only property that is owned individually (i.e., property that is not owned jointly with another or property that has no beneficiary designation). In your Last Will, you select a personal representative or executor to administer your probate estate after your death. The court then supervises the activity of the personal representative and the administration of your estate. It is probably this court oversight that causes people to say probate costs too much, takes too long, and is too public of a process. Actually, probate can have some significant advantages—court oversight being one. A second advantage is the process for identifying and paying creditors—this time period may be considerably shorter than waiting for a state's creditor claim period to run. In Florida, without a probate administration, creditors have two years to file claims against an estate.[24]

If you die with individually owned assets, whether you die with a Last Will or without one (intestate), your estate will be subject to probate. There are essentially three steps in

24 http://www.flsenate.gov/Laws/Statutes/2012/733.2121

the probate process: (1) identify, gather and value the assets of the estate, (2) identify and pay the creditors of the estate (including taxes, attorney fees and personal representative fees, accounting fees and appraisals), and (3) distribute the remaining assets to the beneficiaries (as set forth in your Last Will or as determined by your state's intestate succession rules). The probate court will oversee each of these steps to ensure they are done properly and timely.

If you own assets in more than one state, you may have more than one probate—one for each state where you own property. This may significantly increase the expense and time delays given the need to maneuver through each state's probate process and the hiring of legal counsel in each jurisdiction.

Trusts are effective when signed, and control only the property owned by the trust or the property where the trust is named as beneficiary. With an unfunded trust, you may have both probate administration and trust administration, resulting in unmet expectations by the successor trustee or beneficiaries. In fact, most trusts are unfunded because of the uncertainty and complexity surrounding changing ownership of an asset or the renaming of beneficiaries. This really should be done under the supervision of a legal professional and should be reviewed annually for accuracy.

A trust names a successor trustee to take over the administration of the trust upon your death. You may also name a successor trustee to step in if you become mentally incompetent. The administration of your trust after death is private, but your trustee is still responsible for accounting for your assets, paying your debts, the expenses of trust administration (including taxes, attorney fees and trustee fees) and distributing the assets according to the terms of your trust. This privacy factor can also result in unexpected consequences because untrained successor trustees may not be familiar with state trust laws and may, therefore, administer the estate improperly. Family members may be hesitant to pursue legal action either because they want to avoid family disharmony or they aren't aware there has been a breach of fiduciary responsibility.

Often, the eldest child is named as the successor trustee charged with the responsibility of administering a parent's estate. It is not uncommon for this "uneducated" person with no experience in the world of trust administration to overlook the formalities of administering the trust or assuming the trust assets are now for the sole personal use of the trustee. The privacy aspect of a trust doesn't mean the successor trustee doesn't need legal guidance or assistance but often trustees are reluctant to seek out professional help.

When you consider the cost of administration after death, whether in a probate or trust administration, it is important to also consider the overall cost of estate planning. The cost of estate planning is not just the cost after death—probate, trust administration, legal fees, personal representative or trustees fees, accounting fees, appraisal fees and taxes, to name a few. It's also the initial cost (what you paid the first time you did your planning) and ultimately, the cost of keeping your plan updated over time. In some instances, the failure to keep a plan updated can result in a total failure of the plan—thereby resulting in a loss of 100% of the estate assets. An even bigger cost can be the emotional cost of destroyed family relationships if the plan doesn't work as intended.

Other costs include final expenses related to the disposition of our body—burial or cremation and memorial services. In many states, your heirs have the right to decide whether you are buried or cremated, regardless of the instructions you leave in your Last Will or otherwise. You have the option, however, to pre-plan your burial or cremation and memorial services. While pre-planning will not guarantee your heirs won't still go against your wishes, they may think long and hard about spending additional money and depleting their inheritance.

If you have lost a loved one, you should gather a team to advise you. This team might consist of an attorney, a certified public accountant, a financial advisor, trusted friends and perhaps a professional trustee. The following is recommended:

- Allow yourself the time and luxury to grieve
- Complete funeral and memorial service arrangements
- Contact immediate family and friends
- Locate estate planning documents (these will become your Operating Manual)
- Locate asset and creditor information
- Arrange for the care of surviving family and pets
- Secure real and personal property
- Read the Operating Manual in its entirety (Last Will or Living Trust)
- Gather your Professional Team

There are certain things you don't want to do, and your attorney will be able to properly advise you on those issues. Many of these relate to maximizing estate tax benefits. Your attorney will also be able to advise you on proper notifications to make to governmental agencies and organizations, and also help you with the inventory of assets, identification of creditors, priority of debt payments, and identification of, and distribution to beneficiaries.

As personal representative or trustee, you have a fiduciary responsibility to:

- Comply with the terms of the Last Will or Living Trust
- Comply with the laws relating to wills and trusts
- Be fair in dealings with creditors and beneficiaries
- Comply with tax requirements
- Segregate, preserve and invest estate or trust assets
- Keep and render a full and accurate record and accounting of estate and/or trust assets

Probate administration generally ends when the judge has concluded the personal representative has completed his or her responsibilities, including the payment of all debts and the distribution of assets. Trust administration concludes pursuant to the terms of the trust document— this may be upon outright distribution, or upon distribution when the beneficiaries reach certain ages, when administration is too expensive so as to become "burdensome," or not for many generations because of the existence of continuing trusts.

When considering your own estate plan, it's a good idea to review asset ownership and beneficiary designations and how they integrate with your overall goals and the directions contained in your plan. Make sure your estate plan nominates those individuals or organizations with the greatest opportunity to succeed as personal representative or successor trustee.

Keep your plan current and relevant to your life's ever-changing situation. In addition, consider leaving a heart-felt letter that will allow your loved ones to have one last conversation with you—over and over again.

Co-create your plan with counseling-oriented planning partners so that you are confident all issues have been explored and discussed.

Commit yourself and your family to a formal lifetime maintenance and education program to ensure your plan is relevant at the time it is needed.

Keep your documents and assets organized and tell your loved ones where they can locate important documents in the event of your incapacity and death.

Lastly, secure appropriate assistance for you and your loved ones through the development of a strong relationship with a legal professional to assure your wisdom is transferred along with the rest of your wealth.

What we have done for ourselves alone dies with us; what we have done for others and the world remains and is immortal.

~Albert Pike

Glossary of Estate Planning Terms

Administrator: Person named in your will and appointed by the court to administer your probate estate. Also called an Executor or Personal Representative.

Agent: An individual named in a power of attorney with authority to act on the power giver's behalf. Has a fiduciary responsibility to the power giver. Sometimes called Attorney-in-Fact.

Ancillary Administration: An additional probate in another state. Typically required when you own assets or real estate in a state other than the state where you live that is not titled in the name of your trust or in the name of a joint owner with rights of survivorship.

Applicable Exclusion Amount: The amount of property owned by a decedent effectively exempt from the federal estate and gift tax ($5,340,000 in 2014).

Attorney-in-Fact: An individual named in a power of attorney with authority to act on the power giver's behalf. Has a fiduciary responsibility to the power giver. Sometimes called an Agent.

Basis: What you paid for an asset. Value used to determine gain or loss for capital gains and income tax purposes.

Beneficiary: The person named in a will or trust to receive or benefit from property owned by the maker of the Will or grantor of a Trust. During lifetime, a trust grantor may be a beneficiary.

Buy-Sell Agreement: A written agreement between co-owners of a business to determine the rights of the owners in the event of retirement, termination, bankruptcy, divorce, disability or death.

Capacity: The legal competence to effectively perform a given act (e.g., to write a Will or Trust or enter into a binding contract).

Co-Trustees: Two or more individuals who have been named to act together in managing a trust's assets. A Corporate Trustee can also be a Co-Trustee.

Corporate Trustee: An institution, such as a bank, trust company, or charitable organization that specializes in managing or administering trusts.

Decedent: A person who has died.

Disclaim: To refuse to accept a gift or inheritance so it may be transferred to the next recipient in line. Currently must be done within nine months of the date-of-death to be tax qualified. Sometimes referred to as a "legal no thank you."

Durable Power of Attorney for Financial Matters: A legal directive that gives another person full or limited legal authority to make legal, financial and property decisions on your behalf. May be effective immediately or "springing" depending on your jurisdiction. Valid through mental incapacity or disability. Ends upon revocation, adjudication of incapacity, or death.

Durable Power of Attorney for Healthcare: A legal directive that gives another person legal authority to make health care decisions for you if you are unable to make them for yourself. Also called Healthcare Proxy, Healthcare Surrogate or Medical Power of Attorney.

Estate Administration: The process of settling either a probate estate or trust estate. There are generally three steps that include identifying, gathering and valuing the assets, paying the debts of the estate and distributing the balance to the beneficiaries.

Executor/Executrix: The person nominated in a Will and thereafter appointed by the Probate Court to manage and distribute a decedent's estate in accordance with the terms of the Will. Also known as a Personal Representative.

Fiduciary: Person or entity having the legal duty to act for another person's benefit and occupying a position of trust and accountability. Requires great confidence, trust, and a high degree of good faith. Usually associated with a Trustee, Personal Representative, Executor, Guardian, or Conservator.

Funding: The process of re-titling and transferring assets to your Living Trust. Also includes the re-designation of beneficiaries to include your Living Trust as a beneficiary. Sometimes called asset integration.

Generation Skipping Transfer (GST) Tax: A federal tax imposed on certain transfers, either by gift during life or at death, between a donor/decedent and a person more than one generation removed (e.g., a grandchild).

Gift Tax: Federal tax on completed lifetime gifts made from one person to another. The current lifetime exclusion amount is $5,340,000 for 2014. The current annual exclusion amount is $14,000. May require tax reporting to the IRS on Form 709, a gift tax return.

Grantor: The person who establishes a trust. Also referred to as the "Trustor," "Trustmaker" or "Settlor."

Gross Estate: The total value, for estate tax purposes, of everything one has an ownership interest at the time of death. Includes everything you own, everything you control and everything your name is on.

Guardian: an individual or professional appointed by the Guardianship Court to be responsible for the person or property of a Ward.

Guardianship: A court supervised proceeding whereby after evaluation and review a Guardian is appointed to act on behalf of a minor or incapacitated person (the Ward). A Guardian must be appointed if the incapacitated person did not designate an agent or surrogate in a Durable Power of Attorney (for financial and health care matters) while he or she was competent.

Heir: The person entitled to distribution of an asset or property interest under applicable state law in the absence of a Will. The terms "heir" and "beneficiary" are not synonymous.

Health Care Proxy: A legal document that gives another person legal authority to make health care decisions for you if you are unable to make them for yourself. Also called Durable Power of Attorney for Healthcare, Healthcare Surrogate or Medical Power of Attorney.

Inter vivos: Latin term that means "between the living." An *inter vivos* trust is created while you are living instead of after you die. A Revocable Living Trust is an *inter vivos* trust.

Intestate/Intestacy: When a person dies without a valid will, his or her estate is distributed pursuant to state intestacy laws.

Irrevocable Life Insurance Trust (ILIT): An irrevocable trust for the purpose of holding title to life insurance. Used as an advance planning technique to remove the death benefit proceeds of a life insurance policy from an insured's gross taxable estate. Can be used to take advantage of annual exclusion gifts.

Irrevocable Trust: A trust that cannot be changed, amended or canceled once it is created. Opposite of a Revocable Living Trust created during lifetime.

Intestate: Dying without a Will.

Joint Ownership: When two or more persons own the same asset, either as tenants in common or as joint tenants with right of survivorship.

Joint Tenants with Right of Survivorship: A form of joint ownership where the deceased owner's share automatically and immediately transfers to the surviving joint tenant(s) or owner(s).

Living Trust: A legal entity created during your life, to which you transfer ownership of your assets. Contains your instructions to control and manage your assets while you are alive and well, plan for you and your loved ones in the event of your mental disability and give what you have, to whom you want, when you want, the way you want at your death. Avoids guardianship of property and avoids probate only if fully funded at incapacity and/or death. Also called a Revocable Inter Vivos Trust.

Life Alliance Agreement: A written agreement between two life partners for the purpose of establishing ownership to property, rights and obligations with regard to property and disposition of property in the event of the termination of the relationship.

Life Alliance Partner: A life partner of the same or opposite-sex in a committed, but unmarried, relationship.

Limited Liability Company (LLC): A form of legal entity that can provide limited liability from the claims of creditors. Can be taxed as a sole proprietorship, partnership, s-corporation or c-corporation.

Living Will: A legal document that sets forth your end of life wishes regarding the termination of life-prolonging procedures (respiration, hydration, nutrition) if you are mentally incapacitated and your illness or injury is expected to result in your death.

Personal Representative: Another name for an Executor or Administrator.

Pet Trust: A special trust prepared to ensure your pet receives proper care after you die or in the event you become incapacitated. Contains sufficient funds and instructions to provide lifetime care for your pet. Also names pet caregivers, an Animal Care Panel and Trustees.

Pour Over Will: An abbreviated Will used with a Living Trust. It sets forth your instructions regarding guardianship of minor children and the transfer (pour over) of all assets owned in your individual name (probate assets) to your Living Trust.

Power of Attorney: A legal directive that gives another person legal authority to act on your behalf for a stated purpose. Ends at revocation, incapacity (unless it is a durable power of attorney) or death.

Probate: The legal process of validating a Will, paying debts, and distributing assets after death. Generally requires the services of a qualified attorney.

Probate Estate: The assets owned in your individual name at death (or assets with beneficiary designations payable to your estate). Does not include assets owned as joint tenants with rights of survivorship, pay-on-death accounts, transfer-on-death designations, insurance payable to a named beneficiary or trust, and other assets with beneficiary designations.

Probate Fees: Legal, Executor/Personal Representative, court, and appraisal fees for an estate that requires probate. Probate fees are paid from assets in the estate before the assets are fully distributed to the heirs or beneficiaries.

Revocable Living Trust: Another name for a Living Trust.

Spendthrift Clause: Protects assets in a Trust from a beneficiary's creditors. Prohibits a beneficiary from pledging or borrowing against trust assets.

Successor Trustee: Person or institution named in a trust instrument that will assume responsibility in the event the acting Trustee dies, resigns or otherwise becomes unable to act.

Tangible Personal Property: Personal property that ordinarily has no registered owner, such as furniture, clothing, jewelry, antiques, collections, etc., but not cash or other financial assets.

Tenancy by the Entirety (TBE): A form of joint ownership of property available only to married couples. Very similar to joint tenants with rights of survivorship whereby title to the property automatically vests in the surviving spouse. TBE ownership provides creditor protection in some states.

Tenants in Common (TIC): A form of joint ownership whereby a deceased tenant's share passes to his or her heirs or beneficiaries through his or her estate.

Testamentary Trust: A trust created in a Will or Trust. Only becomes effective at death. May not avoid probate when created in a Will.

Testate: An estate where the decedent died with a valid Will.

Trust Administration: The legal process required to administer trust assets after incapacity or death. Includes the management of trust assets for the named beneficiaries, the payment of debts, taxes or other expenses and the distribution of assets to beneficiaries according to the trust instructions. Generally requires the assistance of an attorney.

Trustee: Person, institution or charitable organization who manages and distributes another's assets according to the instructions in the trust instrument.

Will (or Last Will & Testament): A written document with instructions for disposing of assets after death and appointing a guardian for a minor child. A Will can only be enforced through the probate court.

ABOUT THE AUTHOR

Peggy R. Hoyt, J.D., M.B.A, B.C.S.*

*Florida board certified specialist in Wills, Trusts and Estates and Elder Law

Peggy is an attorney, author and entrepreneur who reflects her passion for pets in almost everything she does. She comes by her love of animals naturally as her father was the President and CEO of The Humane Society of the United States from 1970-1997.

Peggy and her law partner, Randy Bryan, own and operate The Law Offices of Hoyt & Bryan, LLC—Family Wealth & Legacy Counsellors, in Oviedo, Florida. Both Peggy and Randy are dual Florida Bar board certified specialists in Wills, Trusts and Estates as well as Elder Law. Their firm limits its practice to estate planning and elder law issues including the creation, maintenance and administration of estate plans that "work." Areas of expertise also include planning for special needs family members, unmarried couples, business succession and of course, pets.

Peggy has written a number of books. Her first, *All My Children Wear Fur Coats—How to Leave a Legacy for Your Pet,* (LegacyForYourPet.com) was inspired by her pets, currently three horses, seven dogs (including one retired service dog) and two cats. Other co-authored books include *Special People, Special Planning—Creating a Safe Legal Haven for Families with Special Needs; Loving Without a License—An Estate Planning Survival Guide for Unmarried Couples and Same Sex Partners; A Matter of Trust—The Importance of Personal Instructions; Women in Transition—Navigating the Legal and Financial Challenges in Your Life; Like a Library Burning—Saving and Sharing Stories of a Lifetime; Thank Everybody for Everything—Grow Your Life and Business with Gratitude; Gratitude Expressions—a Five Year Journal;* and The Straight Talk Series that includes *Straight Talk! About Estate Planning* and *Straight Talk! What to Do When Some-one Dies.* All are available on Amazon.com.

Peggy is active in a variety of organizations, including WealthCounsel, ElderCounsel, the Academy of Florida Elder Law Attorneys (AFELA), Central Florida Estate Planning Council and as an Executive Council member of the General Practice, Solo and Small Firm Section of the Florida Bar. She is a frequent speaker on estate planning and elder law topics, as well as practice management including team training and marketing.

Peggy is married to Joe Allen and spends her "free" time training for limited distance endurance and competitive trail riding events on her rescue Anglo Arab mare, Heaven.

To learn more or to contact Peggy:
Peggy@HoytBryan.com
HoytBryan.com
PeggyHoyt.com
AnimalCareTrust.com
@PeggyRHoyt
@PetLawyers

Resources

The internet provides access to a vast amount of information. Sorting through what's important and discovering what is relevant for you can be overwhelming. Here are some additional resources to answer your questions.

The Law Offices of Hoyt & Bryan, Oviedo, Florida: HoytBryan.com

All of the following books are also available on Amazon. com:

All My Children Wear Fur Coats—How to Leave a Legacy for Your Pet—LegacyForYourPet.com

Special People, Special Planning—Creating a Safe Legal Haven for Families with Special Needs— SpecialPeopleSpecialPlanning.com

A Matter of Trust—The Importance of Personal Instructions— AmatterofTrust.info

Loving Without a License—An Estate Planning Survival Guide for Same Sex Couples and Unmarried Partners— LovingWithoutALicense.com

Women in Transition—Navigating the Legal and Financial Challenges in Your Life— WomenInTransitionToday.com

Like a Library Burning—Saving and Sharing Stories of a Lifetime—LikeALibraryBurning.com

Straight Talk! About Estate Planning—GratitudePartners.com

Straight Talk! What to Do When Someone Dies—GratitudePartners.com

Whether to Wed, by Scott Squillace—WhetherToWed.com

Government Websites:

SSA.gov

IRS.gov

Estate Planning Checklist

Part 1—Communicating Your Wishes

☐	Do you have a will?
☐	Are you comfortable with the personal representatives and/or trustee(s) you have selected?
☐	Have you executed a health care power of attorney (health care surrogate) and living in the event of catastrophic illness or disability? Are you comfortable with the persons you have selected as your surrogate for decision-making purposes? Do these advance directives contain a HIPAA release?
☐	Have you executed a durable financial power of attorney for the purpose of appointing an agent to handle your financial affairs in the event of your disability? Have you chosen people you have complete trust and confidence in?
☐	Have you considered a revocable living trust to consolidate assets, avoid probate, minimize exposure to estate tax and provide long-term protections for your spouse/partner and other family members, including your pets?
☐	If you have a living trust, have you titled your assets in the name of the trust? Have you named your trust as the primary beneficiary on your contract assets? ie. Insurance policies, annuities, and retirement plans?
☐	If you have a Last Will, Living Trust and other legal directives, have they been reviewed in the last two (2) years to ensure they are consistent with your wishes (your legacy), your current family situation, the status of the law and your attorney's changing experience?

Part 2—Protecting Your Family

☐	Does your Last Will name a guardian for your minor children?
☐	Does your estate plan specifically include provisions to protect your spouse/partner in the event of your death?
☐	Are you sure you have the right amount and type of life insurance to help with survivor income, loan repayment, capital needs and estate-settlement expenses?
☐	Have you considered an irrevocable life insurance trust to exclude the insurance proceeds from being taxed as part of your estate?
☐	Have you considered creating trusts for either your spouse/partner or the family to facilitate life-time gift giving?

Part 3—Helping to Reduce Your Estate and Income Taxes

☐	Do you and your spouse/partner each individually own enough assets for each of you to qualify for the applicable exclusion amounts, currently $5.34 million?
☐	Are both your estate plan and your spouse/partner's designed to take advantage of each of your applicable exclusion amounts, currently $5.34 million?
☐	Are you making gifts to family members that take advantage of the annual gift tax exclusion, currently $14,000?
☐	Have you gifted assets with a strong probability of future appreciation in order to maximize future estate tax savings?
☐	Have you considered charitable trusts that can provide you with both estate and income tax benefits?

Part 4—Protecting Your Business

☐	If you own a business, do you have a management succession plan?
☐	Do you have a buy-sell agreement for your family business interests?
☐	Is your spouse/partner employed by your business? Have you taken all steps necessary to ensure his or her continued participation in the business in the event of your death?
☐	Have you considered a gift program that involves your family-owned business?

www.ingramcontent.com/pod-product-compliance
Lightning Source LLC
Chambersburg PA
CBHW060643210326
41520CB00010B/1720